Groomed For Greatness

HOW TO GET WHAT YOU'RE WORTH AS A FITNESS PROFESSIONAL

BY JONATHAN LAUTERMILCH

DEDICATION

This book is dedicated to my loving wife, Renée, who inspires me every day to wake up, do the work, and inspire others to go out and get what they're worth.

RESOURCES

How could you impact your company with 6-figure templates, business systems, marketing material, and laser-like focus as you network with successful Fit Pros from all around the world?

Fill out an application for our Fit Pro Collective program at https://fitprocollective.com/apply and find out!

TABLE OF CONTENTS

FOREWORD

I live with the belief that everyone has a superpower or a gift that they are BEST suited to share with the world. After being a business owner for over half my life, hiring, training, promoting, and unfortunately firing hundreds of employees within the three companies that I run, I've come to understand that MOST people never choose to lean into those gifts.

It's sad to see someone who has a disadvantage in life never use their tools to unlock their potential as they fail to realize their real purpose. It's sadder still to see someone refuse to lean into what they must do to overcome the obstacles, to become someone of purpose and massive value to others even though they've been given every available tool.

Jonathan grew up in a loving family with every advantage offered by an upper-middle-class lifestyle. As the last of three children, he had an older brother who looked out for him, an older sister who got into trouble with him, and a mom and dad who worked hard to provide a safe and loving environment for him to grow. I know this information for a fact because I am Jonathan's older brother.

You might think writing a foreword for your little brother is easier than writing for people you don't know as well, but it's not. It's harder because there's almost TOO much to share as I have watched Jonathan's growth over the years.

Most of us are born with the ability to hear. For those who can't, it's usually apparent quickly. In our family, we thought everything was normal and didn't understand why toddler Jonathan was so angry all the time. As a baby, he always preferred to play alone, and he never spoke. It wasn't until Jonathan was looking at the TV with his head tilted at the age of two-and-a-half that Mom knew something was wrong.

It all started when Jonathan was born, and he opened his mouth as he was being delivered and breathed amniotic fluid into his lungs. He had to remain in the hospital for a few days as his lungs absorbed the fluid. Along the journey to figuring out what to do about his "slower than average" development, a neurologist told her that he would never graduate high school. Another doctor suggested that he was autistic and wanted to start him on drug therapy.

Thank God our mom is an anti-drug person because if she had taken either of those "professional's" advice, I doubt you'd be reading this today.

Around Jonathan's third birthday, Mom took him to see a speech pathologist because his sounds were slurred. From her recounting, Jonathan would sit in a room with a one-way mirror for Mom to look through and just stare at the floor. Somehow the pathologist was able to cajole Jon into playing the games for her to access more of what he was thinking about, but it wasn't a fun time for him. Once, as Jonathan and Mom were in the parking lot of the pathologist's office before his appointment, Jonathan started banging his head on the pavement in a desperate attempt to let Mom know he wasn't interested in going inside.

Over time, the pathologist began to understand that Jon wasn't mentally impaired in any way. This led to the doctors checking his ears. Lo and behold, he had about three inches of packed ear wax blocking both ears. Yet, the story wasn't over ... but the rest of it is his to tell.

I can tell you this. Jonathan's isolation over the first three years of his life had a MAJOR impact on how I have witnessed him navigate life.

I'd imagine it's quite like living in a world where everything looks black and white to you, with shades of gray in between. When someone asks you to bring a red block, you would pick up four different blocks, trying to get it right. To you, they all seem gray... but... you... keep... getting... it... wrong.

Then, one day, you can SEE! Now, not only do you see the difference between red and green; you can see *all* the variations in between. You can articulate with much more detail because you know what it's like for everything to be the same, and NOW you know how very different everything truly is.

I've been fortunate enough to begin mentoring Jonathan when he was about 12 years old, and I can honestly say that he has taught me more about integrity than any person on the planet. He doesn't mince words, and he KNOWS what he's talking about.

From his years of NOT being able to hear, he has a fine BS detector. More importantly, he doesn't use words to compensate for an inferior work ethic or quality of service. I also believe his "handicap" created his superpower: the ability to create structured systems, that when implemented, create repeatable and scalable results.

He first created them for himself, and now he helps other business owners all over the world get the same results he produced.

What I am most proud of is Jonathan's unwavering faith that he has something to share and his refusal to allow ANYTHING from stopping him from achieving those goals. Jonathan is a champion because he steals excuses away from those who dare to complain about not having a "hand up" in life. He's a living, breathing example of, "If I can do it, anybody can do it."

So, my question is ... will you?

Will you take the time to really listen to what he's sharing inside these pages?

You only have two options here... You can continue to beat your head against the pavement, or you can take what's written inside this book to heart and apply it to your life.

I promise if you do the latter, just like Jonathan did, you'll find that what's on the inside is what can and will set you free to begin living the most elite version of your life. I've personally witnessed him do that, so I know it can happen for you.

Enjoy the read,

Kris Whitehead
Owner, ICONIC Alliance
Coach of 6-9-figure entrepreneurs

Bestselling author, *Becoming Iconic: How to Make Today's Ceiling Tomorrow's Floor*

INTRODUCTION

In this book, you are going to hear a lot of stories from my life about sales, mindset, and all the roadblocks I faced along the way.

However, you will learn about the steps and evolutions I've gone through as a rookie personal trainer, a gym manager, a fitness sales expert, and an online business owner.

It's not easy and will require you to give up who you think you are so you can step into who you were destined to become, but if you are willing to make the commitment to become the greatest version of yourself, I assure you it is quite simple.

Before you turn the page, you should know I arranged the content of this book to maximize your experience. Each chapter contains three sections: 1) The story, 2) The Principle(s), and 3) The Business Application(s). I believe in the strength of storytelling, and I wanted to lay down the facts of what I have been through in my life before I got into the takeaways that will benefit you to remember and apply to your life.

Please don't hesitate to reach out if you have any questions or need coaching services. I look forward to helping you get what you're worth in every area of your life.

What you won't are the techniques and processes I've learned along the way that have made me a top producer in the fitness space. Which is why I've created a separate course/workbook you can go through to sharpen those skills. You can access it for free at https://fitprocollective.com/apply.

I'm also going to share with you a powerful mindset that can literally get you anything you want in life if you're willing to adopt it.

CHAPTER 1

WILL IS GREATER THAN SKILL

"To assert your willpower is simply to make up your mind
that you want something and then refuse to be put off."
—*Phillip Cooper*

If you're reading this book, it means you are willing to invest in yourself.

What I want to share with you is that before you can excel in anything, you have to be willing to develop what I call "a winning willset."

That willset comes from developing your mindset around focus and getting what you want in life. Your willset is developed through a process I call "being groomed for greatness."

That grooming process doesn't happen through things that were given to you; it comes from the struggles you experience in life that help develop you into a better version of yourself. When you lean into those struggles and challenges, you come out the other side closer to what you're truly destined to become.

Before I share the lessons I've learned throughout my life that I believe have been specifically designed for me to go through to reach my highest potential, I need you to understand where I came from. I want you to know the story that led to my understanding of how we're all being groomed for greatness in our own unique ways.

My story begins on July 30th, 1985, on a Tuesday evening in a small hospital in Lynchburg, Virginia—the day I was born.

I wasn't supposed to be born for another 30 days and had entered the world at just eight months, one month premature.

My family always jokes that I came out of the oven a little bit too soon. They say that I probably needed to stay in for that extra month, and that's why I came out the way I am.

I couldn't wait to take the world on and go get what I'm worth. Being premature was my first challenge.

The second challenge I faced upon entering the world was swallowing a very large amount of amniotic fluid. This caused several health issues. I had to stay in the ICU for a week as my family gathered around me and prayed for my survival. Fortunately, it all worked out; otherwise, I wouldn't have written this book.

WHY DOES IT MATTER?

I share those challenges I faced at the beginning of my life because many times, when we encounter difficulties, we think, *why me?*

I can answer that question by saying that's what has formed and shaped who I am. Now, I am truly grateful for how things turned out and the opportunity I have to share all the struggles I have gone through with you.

My newborn health scares made up the great beginning of this game called life. In the coming years, I would endure more struggles.

As the typical child grows up in their formative years, they thirst to develop their ability to communicate, understand, and interact with the world around them by the age of two. This is when they can start coherently speaking. But this was not the case for me. My parents noticed that I couldn't speak, and I didn't respond when others spoke to me. Thus began a barrage of doctor visits.

After being dragged to multiple doctor's appointments, the medical opinions all came back to one diagnosis; the doctor told my mother that she and my dad needed to prepare to parent a developmentally handicapped child.

Fortunately, my mother refused to believe the doctors and said, "I'm going to find a doctor who sees what I see when I see my son, no matter what."

When my mother took me to an ear doctor, he discovered the source of my underdevelopment was a build-up of earwax that prevented me from hearing.

I look back on that time, and it seems a little funny that something so minor could have such a large impact on my ability to learn, connect, and understand the world around me.

Once I had a diagnosis, my mother hired one of the top speech therapists in the area, and I began the hard work of learning how to speak through communication rehabilitation. Dr. Jano forever changed my life. My mother took me for weekly assessments, and at the time, it was the last thing that I wanted to do.

I'd built a comfort zone around me. I was used to being left alone, and I became quite okay with that. However, when I saw Dr. Jano, I was constantly being forced out of my comfort zone to learn skills that were very difficult for me.

Dr. Jano was skilled at finding a way to make my therapy sessions fun. She built on my experiences and convinced me to stick with it. After a year of speech therapy, I was speaking full sentences and could carry on entire conversations with people!

This was my first life lesson. I learned that through hard work, you can conquer even the greatest challenges set in front of you. Little did I know that this would be a reoccurring theme throughout my life, and it would eventually lead to speaking and communication becoming a superpower of mine.

WHAT'S THE POINT?

Rarely will facing challenges be what we want to do. Whatever we are dreading is typically what we *have* to do. In my case, I *had* to attend these weekly sessions. It wasn't an option not to go. As a bonus, I not only learned how to speak, but I also learned to communicate with the people around me, which is ironically what I do today for a living.

I get to coach clients all around the world. And because speech was a huge struggle for me, it's given me a unique perspective when it comes to sales and influence.

Everything I've shared in this book was generated through my challenges, becoming intentional, and understanding language through a step-by-step process.

Therapy enabled me to start speaking by the age of three. Although I had made awesome strides, I was still a year behind other kids. And I was behind the curve in a lot of different areas in my life, such as when it came to building relationships, understanding others, and developing empathy. I was behind the curve in my ability to articulate what I was feeling and thinking at any moment.

**That struggle forged what would become
an incredible willset for me.
Notice I said "willset" and not "skillset."**

My willset has helped me put intention behind the skillset needed to attain the lifestyle I've always wanted.

DEVELOPING WILLSET

As I noted in the Introduction, every chapter in this book has been arranged in three sections: 1) The Story, 2) The Principle, and 3) The Application.

As you read through the story sections and learn about each new skill, ask yourself: what are some areas in your life where you can develop a skill you need? What skills could you fine-tune to make your life better? Most importantly, are you willing to develop the right mindset in connection with these goals to make sure you win? Regardless of whether you have talent or even skill, it means little to nothing if it isn't backed by sheer will. We may not be able to control whether we have talent, but we can control our ability to develop skills by engaging in what I call "Doing the work."

You want to aim for this goal. Because when we do the work, we have limitless potential in any area we focus on.

Skills need to be honed. Take the example of sales. Many people think salespeople are born with the gift of sales. But I am not a natural-born salesman. I had to work on my skills and improve my ability to sell. Your success hinges on the work you've put into developing your skills. Stay focused on your development, and you can truly become whoever you want to be. This is the beginning of the path toward greatness.

I believe every challenge in our life is specifically placed there so we can use it as an opportunity to step closer to who we're meant to become.

THE PRINCIPLES

I've identified five main points for you to take away from the story I shared about my tough start in life.

1. **What to do when a roadblock gets in the way of what we want**. When I was a toddler, I wanted to talk, but I couldn't. Now that I'm older and have a little perspective, I know there are times in life when we want things, but before we can have them, we have to conquer the roadblocks standing in our way. If we want to get past these roadblocks—whatever they might be—we have to first identify them. We have to face them head-on. Not being able to speak was a pretty obvious roadblock. It created a tremendous desire in me to overcome it. After all, it's pretty freaking important to learn how to talk to people.

2. **Why you need to increase your skill level.** To keep up with the other kids my age, I had to increase my skill levels. That was my path to success. As we know, not everyone is blessed with talent. I'd love to be a professional basketball player, but that's not what God put in the cards for me. Yet, I *can* control my desire to work on the skills I do have that can get me to where I want to be in life. Learning how to speak turned into public speaking, posting on social media, selling, working with clients, and voicing my message around the world. I drilled into the skills I needed to work on. What are your skills?

3. **Why you need core beliefs and ideologies.** Before I tell you the third takeaway, I need you to understand something. When we are between the ages of three to seven, we adopt our core beliefs and ideologies about the world. These can be good beliefs. They can be bad beliefs. Nonetheless, they are the beliefs we tend to carry into our adult years.

   I wasn't supposed to be successful. I wasn't supposed to be good at sales. My first three years when I was learning how to speak was only the beginning. When I developed negative beliefs about myself, it impacted the next three to seven years of my life. Thankfully, my positive beliefs were my saving grace. They gave me the willingness to put in the effort and work.

   As you read through this book and reflect on your life, think about the limiting beliefs you developed at an early age through your challenges. Are these beliefs impacting your life now? If so, get clear on what those beliefs are. I don't want you to worry if you're facing roadblocks because I'm going to help you build ramps over those roadblocks as we move throughout this book.

4. **Why you need to know anyone can do it.** It's ironic that after my late start, I now get paid to talk to people. So, when I tell you that if I can do it, you can do it, I mean it... I believe it. This belief is absolutely authentic and comes from the bottom of my heart. I know it's true because I

accomplished goals that were unlikely based on my obstacles. Not many people in my circle thought I could ever change the trajectory of my life. They had a hard time seeing all that was possible for me. Since coming through that experience, I have absolute confidence and faith that you can plow through your roadblocks, too.

5. **What does the greatness path look like for you?** First, ask yourself: what are the main struggles you're having? How can you apply the mindset of "will versus skill" to defeat them? Whether you're dealing with self-sabotage, not being good at sales, or anything else, you must know your weak spots and triggers. Figure out what they are, then you can work on them.

   As you explore this concept, discover what happens when you work through the rough times in your life instead of just accepting them. As you build ramps to drive over your roadblocks, you'll learn your roadblocks are stepping stones to take you from good to great.

THE BUSINESS APPLICATIONS

One of the themes present through this book is the consistency of one's actions, or what I call "How you do one thing is how you do everything." My journey as a newborn and the struggle I went through with physical therapy greatly influenced how I operate in the world. These trying times would serve as the catalysts for the success I am now experiencing at the age of thirty-six.

1. **Discipline your mindset for your business.** If you want to grow, you need to consistently work on areas where you want to grow. You can become great in any area of your business if you have a mindset that fuels the work to develop the skills you need. When it comes to using any skill successfully, remember that success is equal to 80% will and 20% skill.

   You can have all the tactics, tools, and shiny objects, but if you don't have the discipline to develop your mindset, you won't achieve the results you're striving for. As you get clear on the different areas of your life that need improvement, identify how you will put your discipline into action.

2. **Go get what you're worth.** This is the mission statement for several of my companies. But let's get clear. When most people hear, "Go get what you're worth," they think of sales. Is that you? Do you think of income? Your mission? Building your business? What about living the lifestyle of your dreams? If your answer was, "yes, yes, yes, and yes", that's awesome! But when you dig deep into the mindset and philosophy that empowers you to get what you're worth, you'll find it's actually about the commitments you have made to yourself. These commitments exist in all areas of your life. Are you getting what you're worth in your finances? In your physical health? In your relationships? In your friendships? Who are you supposed to be? And who have you always thought you

would become? "Getting what you're worth" is ultimately about stepping into the best version of yourself by following through on your commitments.

3. **Success Equals Taking Inventory.** When you truly embrace the will behind the skill, you become an unstoppable force. You can get whatever it is you set your mind to achieve. As you travel along that path, take inventory of those around you.

    If my mother hadn't believed in me and hadn't been willing to take me to the doctor, I never would've gotten to a place where I have a beautiful family of my own and the opportunity to do what I believe I was put on this planet to do through multiple businesses with clients spanning seven countries. My mother took me from doctor to doctor until we finally found Dr. Jano, my speech therapist—this is the main reason I'm speaking to you right now.

    You need to have the right people who add value in your circle, too. But you might already have people in your life who do that for you—as you do that for them. These people can help us lean farther into what we need to improve so we can get what we're worth. We may also have people who serve as detractors. These people pull away from us as they see us move forward and experience success. These people don't support us. It's important to know the roles people play in our lives, so take inventory of those around you. When you put your will behind any-thing and everything you do, you will see who's with you for the long haul and who's only hanging around for the short term.

ASK YOURSELF...

- What kind of life do you want to have?

- Do you want to be healthy and fit?

- Do you want to have a six-figure business?

- Do you want to have a seven-figure business?

- Do you want eight figures?

- Will you have a large team?

- Will you have a small team?

- Do you want to run your company?

- Did you build a company so someone else can run it while you remain the owner?

- Do you want to spend your time when you want, how you want?

- If so, what does that life look like to you?

Get super clear on what you want when it comes to your goals and ambitions.

These are critical questions to answer if you want to move forward. You must know what you want. To get even clearer, click the link and use the promo code GREATNESS247 to get the *Groomed for Greatness* training for FREE:

https://jonathanlautermilch.com/training.

These trainings will walk you through specific questions that allow you to identify your roadblocks and apply practical strategies to build ramps over them.

If you're a fit pro or a gym owner reading this book, I created two companies dedicated to helping people just like you overcome mental roadblocks and reach success in all areas of life.

To apply for our programs and learn more about what we do, how the programs work, and most importantly if we're a good fit to help you grow your active client base, visit the application link: https://fitprocollective.com/apply.

Answer a few short questions, and one of our team members will reach out to you. This isn't a sales call. We simply want to explore your goals and where you are in relation to them. If you're a fit and we're a fit, we'll customize a plan to help you reach your highest potential.

CHAPTER 2

IF YOU CAN CLOSE LOVE, YOU CAN CLOSE SALES

"How you do one thing is how you do everything."
—Zen Buddhism"

When most people think of the word sales, they envision money or a time when someone got one over on them. What I'm about to share with you is going to rewire your mindset to what sales really is.

Sales is simply persuasion.

You're persuading someone to live a better life, persuading them to make better choices for themselves, or even persuading them to buy into you and your ideas. We are all wired to be sales-people. We were built to persuade others of our ideas and beliefs —this tendency comes from our very biology.

THE ONE FORCE THAT DRIVES US ALL... SEX ...

At a very young age, like most boys, my main focus in my life was to find a girl.

Little did I know, it would be through this pursuit that I would begin sharpening my sales skills.

Let me explain what I mean by sharing two stories with you about the two loves of my life who taught me invaluable lessons.

MY FIRST REAL LESSON ON HIGH TICKET SALES...

Theresa was the first love of my life. I was 16 years old and a sophomore in high school when I first laid eyes on her. I was attracted to her immediately. She had brown hair, brown eyes, worked out every single day, and it showed. Now, at the time, she was way out of my league. And I mean, waaaay out of my league. I was a sophomore while she was a junior, and she was one of the cool kids at school. I had just moved to her school and was still making friends and getting used to my new surroundings.

I first saw her when we were in homeroom. I was terrified to talk to her for a month. Over the next couple of months, she awkwardly caught me gazing at her from across the room. We finally had a conversation when the teachers paired us together for a project. Through that project, Theresa gave me the opportunity to get to know her better, and we were able to hang out with common friends. This led to us being out alone a couple of times. After that, I got my nerve up to ask her on an actual date. As I sat there in terror waiting for her response, she smiled and nodded back, "Sure."

This would be one of the first sales I'd ever make, and it would initiate my addiction to winning. Funnily enough, later on, she would ask me why I didn't ask her out sooner.

It took me so long to ask her out because I was terrified of being rejected. Before her, I hadn't had much luck with the ladies.

Now, don't get me wrong. I'd dated before Theresa, but it was never like it felt with her. Before I asked her on a date, something inside me changed; it pushed me to go. I thought, *if I don't ask for it, I'll regret it for the rest of my life*. From that pitch and the courage to ask for that first date, we wound up being in a five-year relationship—and that alone taught me a boatload of lessons.

How many times have you been across the table from a client and felt terrified to ask for the sale? How many times have you met your dream client only to be too scared to ask for the opportunity for their business? Remember, if you don't ask, you'll never get your dream girl, your dream guy, or your dream client.

HOW MY WIFE TAUGHT ME THE LONG GAME WHEN IT CAME TO SALES

The second lady in the story is actually the most important lady in my life today; my wife, Renée. Renée and I met 11 years ago in a pretty funny way. We were personal trainers at the same gym. At the time, I'd been working as a personal trainer for two years, so I had a little bit of experience. But you would never know it by the looks of me or by the way I spoke. I hid it very well. When Renée was recruited to the gym by our general manager, I had an opportunity to get to know her.

Renée was recruited because she was the eye of the gym. Every staff member knew her, and all the guys wanted to be with her.

I watched each of my fellow colleagues make their pitch and bomb as they clearly overlooked the universal signs a woman sends at the gym when she wants to be left alone. Ball cap pulled down, headphones on, and a resting bitch face that could freeze hell over.

As I watched Renée reject them one by one, I knew I would have to go about getting close to her using a very different angle. When I looked at Renée, I knew this was the woman I didn't just want to be with; I wanted to spend the rest of my life with her.

**As Renée and I got to know each other,
we quickly found out we were both highly
competitive and self-proclaimed alphas.**

We didn't actually like each other much within the first month. She thought I was a cocky asshole, and I thought she was a feminazi. That's when Renée challenged me to a month-long sales contest and said she "was going to kick my ass and I was going to have to change gyms." As we competed head-to-head in that contest with the whole team watching, we were back to back, and neck and neck. I would be up one day. She would be up the next. Then as we hit the final days, she blasted past me in the numbers. I thought for sure I was going to lose and prepared to swallow my pride regardless of how painful that was going to be. As we reached the final day of the month, I was wrapping up with my last client for the day. It was a Friday at six o'clock. My head dropped, my shoulders slumped; I knew in mere minutes I was going to have to admit defeat to my adversary ... until my client saw one of our training specials. She walked up to me and asked, "What's the Buy 20, Get 10 Free special all about?"

As I tried to hide my excitement from the client, I put my arm around her and said, "That is a fantastic question! Let's go over here, and I'll walk you through it." I led my client over to the membership area, and as I looked back over my shoulder, I could see Renée and our fitness manager shaking their heads. I ever so humbly flipped Renée the bird as I walked into the sales pit to claim victory with a smug smirk on my face. Little did I know it wouldn't be the sales contest that I actually won; it would be her respect.

I tell you that story to illustrate the point that our relationship started with us not liking each other and being adversarial, but it led to common respect. We saw what the other was doing. We saw the grind and hustle we put into growing our business that month. When the contest was over, everyone won.

Our friendship led to us hanging out outside the gym. It was six months from that point until I convinced Renée to go on our first date. I don't think I've ever worked that hard for a sale in my life, but it would teach me something I would take with me throughout the rest of my sales career.

We've spent the last 11 years together, and she's my best friend and the love of my life. She is exactly who I wanted to spend my time with. Yes, it did take me six months to get that first date. If you break it down, that's a lot of sales marketing. That's a lot of good sales follow-up. In retrospect, I can see I didn't have the right offer for her when I was courting her, which is why it took six months longer to go on that first date than I would have liked. But I was resilient and persistent in keeping my eye on what I truly wanted, which was to have a lifelong relationship with her.

I'm sure you're thinking, why is he sharing dating stories, analogies, and a sales tip in a personal development book?

Because this supports what I shared with you earlier; that "how we do one thing is how we do everything." We're all biologically wired to want to have one special person in our life, whoever that might be. That's the origin of our sales ability, knowing that we are all designed to be salespeople. We're inherently gifted to be salespeople, so we don't just create success in business, but so we can have love and happiness. That's how we've gotten this far as a species. That's why I know what I teach works. It is built on instinct. If you can find love, I can show you how to grow your business.

THE PRINCIPLES

Like I said, if you can close love, you can close sales. Now, if you're a 40-year-old virgin, you may need a little bit more help than someone else reading this book. I'm not a relationship guru, but when it comes to developing relationships that turn into sales, I'm your guy.

1. This is the main point that I want you to take away after reading this chapter: you have at your disposal every-thing you need to sell. You have the right instinct. You just have to be willing to tap into it.

    I'm not only talking about what you need to do to close the initial sale. What I am teaching you covers everything relating to sales, like following up and overcoming object-tions. Getting my first date with my wife took a lot of follow-up and understanding of what my objective would be over a specific timeframe. As I navigated those six months, I knew that my end goal was to get a date with Renée, and I also knew that was going to happen. I was very confident about what I brought to the table in terms of a relationship.

2. **You must be willing to do the not-so-fun parts of sales.** You have to commit to the follow-up process. You have to understand someone's objections and how to navigate those appropriately.

3. **You first have to be willing to ask for what you want, whether it's in your personal or business life.**

4. **Finally, you also have to be willing to work for it.**

THE BUSINESS APPLICATIONS.

If you were paying attention as I was sharing these stories with you, then you can connect the dots. What I just taught you is 100% applicable to all kinds of businesses.

When I wanted to get the girl, I had to firmly understand who she was, where she was coming from, and most importantly, what she was looking for.

---

1. **Apply this exact tactic to your business: Understand your client on a damn-near romantic level**. When you understand them, where they're at, where they want to go, and what their mental roadblocks are, then you can strategize how to provide the ramp they need to get over those roadblocks. Think about the process you go through in building relationships with your customers so you can earn their business. Is your sales process focused on getting what you want? Or is it designed to create so much value that the client truly wants what you offer? Anyone can have a one-night stand when it comes to business. The secret is in finding the clients who want to do life with you and having a process that takes them from prospect to lifer.

   Once I got that first date with Renée, things were smooth sailing. With Teresa, I didn't have to follow up for six months, but I had to go on multiple dates before we got to that point.

You will also need to figure out the fastest courting system to move your clients and prospects down the path to getting into a business relationship with you.

2. **Provide value and understand that that value is in the eye of the beholder**. Theresa and Renée saw totally different values in me. I had to understand that the value they saw was what allowed me to move our relationship forward.

   What is the value your clients see in you? Understand I am not asking about how valuable your offerings are in your business. I want you to know, in terms of what you do, what your client sees as valuable. I want you to know how that value impacts their life—which is where all buying decisions come from.

3. **Go deep versus wide in your business**. If you haven't noticed by now, I'm much more of a long-term relationship kinda man in every area of my life. I'd rather take my time and do the work to build deep relationships with those I do business with so I don't have to constantly look for new clients over and over again.

   The same mistakes that plague romantic relationships happen in business relationships. Those looking for a one-night stand never find love. Those who quit and leave right before the relationship is about to blossom never find love. The same goes for those who are in sales. The clients looking for the one-night-stand in business have to constantly be on the hunt for the next one. But there is still an opportunity for this client to want to have a relationship with you. You just have to be willing. Salespeople who aren't willing to follow up and take part in an in-depth process to move their potential client to a buying decision will always have to wait and look for new opportunities.

When you apply a step-by-step sales process in your business, you can go deep versus wide in your prospects. When you use this strategy, you will increase your ROI more than you can measure.

Here's a scenario that provides a clear example. When you first get a lead, instead of pitching them right away, qualify them via text message or through a DM (direct message). After you qualify them, *then* you move them to a 20-30-minute meet and greet call to gain more clarity on their needs and goals.

From that call, you will have a clear idea of who this person is, what they want, and what they need. If it seems like a great fit, you can move them to a presentation call where you demonstrate the value you will add when you solve their problem.

Having a courting system in place will dramatically overhaul your business. You will need fewer leads to get the ROI you're used to.

CHAPTER 3

THE STRUGGLE IS WHAT MAKES *YOU STRONG*

*"Show me someone who has done something worthwhile,
and I'll show you someone who has overcome adversity.
–Lou Holtz"*

Life has a funny way of building you up before it breaks you down, only to build you back up again.

In between 2004 and 2008, I attended Radford University, where I received my sports medicine degree.

As I was growing up, the true sign of success in my family was pursuing academics. It didn't matter if I received a master's or doctoral degree. The goal was to earn a degree.

Early on, I was set on a path to become a physical therapist. It complemented my interests well. I had been into fitness, health, and working out while I was growing up.

Between 2004-2008, I would dive into my physical therapy undergrad program that helped me understand what my life would look like as a physical therapist. I was forever turned off from physical therapy when I took a special populations training class. Don't get me wrong, it's a demographic that needs help, and there are tons of great coaches I've met over the years who thrive on helping that community. But I knew I would be absolutely miserable every single day for the rest of my life in that line of work.

As I entered my final year in college, I had to make a decision about what I wanted to do for the rest of my life. I could study and attempt to pass my doctoral program exam and continue on that route (which I had no interest in). Or I could capitalize on an opportunity from my brother to do my internship at a very large gym chain—let's call it Cobalt Gym—in one of their franchise locations in Virginia.

It was a no-brainer for me because I already loved the gym and knew what the power of fitness had done for me in my life.

After graduating college, I did my internship at Cobalt's. It was a small mom-and-pop franchise operation, and I worked there for free for three months—but I loved every second of it.

In my internship, I did all the dirty work that none of the employees wanted to do. You name it; I did it. Cleaning the bathroom, racking the weights, cleaning the weight room, showing gym members how to use the equipment, checking people in at the front desk, shadowing trainers, so on and so forth—I did it all.

Through those three months at Cobalt's, and after a lot of hard work, I earned an invitation to work as a personal trainer. To say I was ecstatic would be an understatement. Throughout that time, I had fallen in love with the culture of fitness and the impact I could have on people's lives, as well as the perceived freedom to manipulate my schedule and personal income.

The first meeting I ever attended as a personal trainer consisted of five other trainers and me. Three of them were fairly new and had started ahead of me. I was the newest trainer there. We were going over a sales training on how to build our client base.

THEN THEY THREW A PHONE BOOK AT ME

I'll never forget how our manager threw a phone book down on the table and told us that if we wanted to be successful, we had to get comfortable cold calling people to invite them to the gym.

My initial thought was, I didn't go to college and spend $50,000 on a sports medicine degree to work at a gym and cold call people from a fucking phone book! But I soon realized it was my only option. Besides, my fellow trainers dove right into the book and made the calls. If they were doing it, I would give it my best effort, too.

After a couple of days of cold calling people from the Yellow Pages, I quickly realized there had to be a better way. So, I walked up to my manager and asked, "Karen, do we have a list of our current members who have never bought personal training? And do we have a list of former members or former training clients who used to train with us but aren't currently?"

She thought a moment, then replied, "Yes, I can get that for you." She then went to create the list. Before long, she brought it to me. As I laid my eyes on the list, I thought about how it was literal gold. This would be my path to salvation. It would save me from having to cold call people from a phone book. I took about half the pages of the list for myself and left the other half for the rest of the trainers to fight over.

As I went through the list, I reached out to the members who had never worked with a trainer before and invited them to come in so I could give them a personal training session. I also reached out to former clients, inquiring how their experience had been so far and asking what we could do to help them moving forward.

Through that process, I started booking consultations for myself. In my eyes, these appointments were paid dating opportunities. As I booked people to come in and took them through personal training sessions, I worked on building value for them by moving them forward.

That's when I realized the one skill college never taught me: how to sell.

I was one of the worst salesmen you could ever imagine. I said the wrong thing at the wrong time, was afraid to mention the price, and was scared to death of offering people the chance to work with me. My confidence in getting results wasn't high because everything I'd ever learned had been from a textbook. I didn't have any life experience when it came to coaching someone.

That process was grueling, and I almost quit three times. If it hadn't been for my brother, Kris, talking me out of it, there's a good chance I would have quit and wouldn't have written this book you're reading right now!

Fortunately, I didn't quit. I leaned into the challenge because I didn't want to let my brother down.

After each failed opportunity, I would rerun what had happened during the consultation and how I could improve. I would even talk with other trainers and shadow the trainers who were successful in sales. I absorbed what they said, what they did, and how they acted. I learned if I wanted to be successful, I needed to model what successful trainers did.

It was a long road to getting my first consultation. I pitched 39 prospects before I was told "yes" on the 40th try. My first sale was to two college girls from an all-girls school. To be honest, I don't think they bought training from me because of my expertise, but most likely because they thought I was a nice guy who would be fun to work out with.

Closing my first sale was one of the best feelings in the world. It sparked sales, becoming one of my biggest addictions to this day.

But if it wasn't for that first sale, I would have never experienced what was possible. I could have never created a lifestyle where I get paid to help people become a better version of themselves. I want you to remember, as you think about your efforts and dedication, that it took me 39 rejections before I got my first sale. Are you willing to find 39 ways not to do something just to find the one way to make it work?

That first sale kicked off my obsession with sales.

I'd never been taught sales in school, when getting my certification, or even as an employee of a gym. I had to learn it through relentless effort and refusing to give up before I got my first opportunity that helped me see what was possible.

Sales was my biggest struggle in life. It's now my superpower. I get to teach coaches, businesses, and CEOs around the world how to maximize their sales process so they can change more lives and impact their bank account.

When most people first get into sales, they are not naturally gifted. They are awkward, to the point of being damn near uncomfortable—like I was.

If I can lean in and become an expert in fitness sales, then anyone can master fitness sales to get what they want out of their career.

THE PRINCIPLES

1. **Mental toughness**. The long process of closing my first consultation showed me my mental toughness and who I could be. The money had little to no impact on me. I discovered it's very easy to do what we need to when we're accepted. But it's hard to do what we need to when we're constantly rejected.

I can't tell you how many times I thought about quitting. I can't tell you how many times I questioned the decision to become a personal trainer instead of a physical therapist, like my family always wanted me to be. What I can tell you is that my very first experience with fitness would become the foundation on which I built my mindset on how I approach life.

2. **Think about those areas in your life where you're facing resistance, where you're experiencing rejection, where you feel like you're beating your head against the wall, where you're having a hard time breaking through.** Then just feel secure that you will be okay. The best part about sales and business is that you only have to get it right one time to drastically change your life. You won't beat your head against the wall forever.

THE BUSINESS APPLICATIONS

Think about what your struggles are in sales. After every rejection I received when I was trying to close consultations, I would run what I call a "highlight reel" in my head. I would start to break down what happened throughout the process and ask myself: *what went well?* Most importantly, I asked myself *what didn't go well?* This highlighted what I needed to focus on, practice, and the areas I had to strengthen. When I engaged in this process, I didn't have the same issues surface in my next opportunities.

1. **What you want to do the least is what you need to do the most.**

   I had learned everything I thought I needed to learn to be a personal trainer. I learned about the science of the body, nutrition, behavior change, how the gym worked, how to design a program, and how to coach clients. But I was never taught how to make a sale. When it comes to changing lives, you can't truly help someone through your service before the exchange of money.

   ### Leaning into what I wanted to do the least set me free and changed my life.

   ---

2. When you lean into and own your challenges, you will break through whatever obstacle stands in your way. There's a big difference between knowing what to do and actually doing it.

   I realized if I was going to reach my goals, it was up to me. No one else was going to save me. No one else was going to help me. Sure, I had resources around me, but that wasn't enough. It was my job to put those resources to work and figure out how to get where I wanted to go and do what I wanted to do, which was build my client base.

   What do you want to grow toward?

   What challenges do you have?

What do you need to accomplish your goals? And what tasks or actions do you need to own to become successful?

3. **Energy flows where your attention goes**. Often in life and business, it's easy to focus on the problems and struggles. It takes real strength to focus on the wins.

   When you focus on what's going right, it puts you in a place of gratitude. When you're in a place of gratitude, you can see more opportunities. When you see more opportunities, you can see more victories in your life and business. What areas are you struggling in? How are they holding you back? And are you leaning into them?

4. **Get clear on what you're great at and honest about what your areas of opportunity are**. Whether it's marketing, lead generation, sales, or even service, there are four main buckets you have to get great at. Part of developing and growing your business is learning there are different skills for each level—no matter if you're a solopreneur, entrepreneur, CEO, investor, etc.

   When you are in this phase, get clear and honest with yourself. Ask yourself, *is this a skill I need to develop and lean into*? Or *can I outsource what's needed to someone else with a different set of skills*? When you delegate your tasks, you can stay in your genius zone. The genius zone happens when you work on what you naturally do well.

5. **The best investment you can ever make is in yourself.** The government can't tax it, and you're guaranteed an ROI if you do the work. No one can take your skills from you. When you invest in your development, not only will you improve—you'll be able to help more people.

As we close this chapter, remember, there are two different types of investments you can make in life: the investment in yourself and the investment in others.

Both investment types will raise you up as you level up so you can continue to get what you're worth and create opportunities to help others get what they're worth. When you focus on the skills required to grow, you'll gain those skills forever. Once again, the best part is **the government can't tax it**.

CHAPTER 4

MY 10,000 HOURS TO SALES MASTERY

"It takes 10,000 hours of intensive practice
to achieve mastery of complex skills."
—*Malcolm Gladwell*

It's easy to think you're a big fish when you're swimming around in a tiny pond.

When I left the gym where I'd gotten my very first sale and had built up a solid book of business for myself, I went to a small franchise location and became one of the top producers. That gave me a big head. Of course, I didn't understand the concept of putting in 10,000 hours to master sales at the time. But I was about to learn that lesson the hard way.

No matter what you're trying to master in your life, it will take countless hours and repetition to develop a high level of skill. In this chapter, I'm going to share the four biggest lessons I learned throughout my 10,000 hours of sales mastery. Most sales gurus would break down their secret process and the psychology of buying, selling, and influencing. Those are all great things to learn and know, and I do have training on these topics you can access, but that's not what this book is about. My purpose in writing this book is to talk about the all-encompassing mindset that is required to really excel in sales and how to go get what you're worth in every area of your life.

After my time at Cobalt Gym in Virginia, I was given an opportunity to move in with my best friend from high school, Ryan, in North Carolina, where he was finishing up his last year of college. I figured I could work at the Cobalt Gym down there and continue to train clients. The bonus was that I could also party it up with him and do what young guys do.

The truth is, I wasn't ready to grow up yet.

I was scared of becoming an actual adult, so I took my opportunity to play around for another year and make a few bucks along the way. Then I packed all my stuff, moved south, and got another job at a Cobalt Gym. Once I arrived, I went to work to rebuild my business. Fortunately, I had learned some valuable lessons about building my business from my first job at the gym.

THE LESSONS

1. I knew the tactics and strategies to find the right people to have conversations with, from current members to former clients.

2. In my first year at the gym, I learned to have very high enthusiasm for what I did. Truth be told, I wasn't the most confident when I asked for the sale. But the one asset I had in spades was that I was high on life and excited to help people. It was my one saving grace that allowed me

to build a book of business. People could feel the enthusiasm coming from me, which in turn, drew them to want to work with me.

I encourage you to become extremely passionate about what you do because if you're not excited about what you do, why the hell should your prospect or client be excited?

Lesson number two didn't pan out as much as I'd hoped. As I built my business, I realized that even though I was having sales conversations with people and had tons of enthusiasm, I was still not growing at the speed I wanted to grow.

It didn't help that the gym wasn't a family environment where people were more open and trusting. This gym was in a rougher area of the neighborhood where I lived. Everyone's guards were up. It forced me to find an answer to the question: "How do I get people to open up so we can have an honest conversation about me helping them?"

That's when I devised to add value upfront, which left the door of opportunity wide open for me.

I had to create quick wins for the people I wanted to help. And I don't mean a win that would change their life, but a win that would change their day. *What were small things I could do to help someone move forward just a little bit faster and a little bit farther than where they were that day? How could I give it to them for free?* I got to work and quickly built a reputation as the go-to guy for corrective exercise. Finally, my $50,000 degree started to pay for itself.

I created an offer for a 30-minute "move better and feel better" session where I'd do a quick assessment and then show the client 2-3 things that helped them move and feel better than when they walked in the door.

Little did I know I had just created my first funnel, and *I was the funnel.*

The discovery that I could get what I wanted by giving others what they wanted first forever changed how I do business.

WHAT A RUSH

During this time, I'd also started dating a girl. She had gone to the same college my friend attended and had just graduated. So, we had a decision to make. Do we part ways as she was moving back home to Knoxville, Tennessee, or do we take the next step and move in together? Once again, I would ask myself the question, *do I want to wonder what could have been?*

So, I quit my job and moved to a new state with no friends or family. All I took with me were the skills I had developed for building a new book of business.

In Tennessee, I had to find a new gym to work at and rebuild my clientele. After checking out all the different gyms and studios, I landed on a company called The Bolt Gym and Fitness.

The funny part about this story is that this company had a location in North Carolina. Several people had suggested to me that I should work there. Back then, my perception was that the gym wasn't for me; it was extremely colorful (it looked like a Chuck E. Cheese). I wrote it off thinking I was more of a Cobalt's Gym kind of guy.

At the time, The Bolt was the only real gym chain in town. I had no choice but to go there to see if I could get a job. After three weeks of following up with the manager every few days and personally driving out there to get an interview, I was finally given an opportunity. Then I was offered a job. Little did I know I would be there for the next five years and would be put through the grinder when it came to my personal and professional development. Working at The Bolt would have an everlasting impact on me personally and professionally.

The Bolt was the first corporate gym I'd ever worked at. Every location previously had been a small mom-and-pop franchise gym. Those gyms didn't have systems. They didn't have real accountability over their employees. It was almost like the wild west where you could make your own rules.

As I got indoctrinated into The Bolt culture, I quickly realized that I didn't know jack shit when it came to business. When I humbled myself and started to learn from others in the organization, I learned the next lesson that would change my life and countless others' lives forever. I continue to teach it to this day.

THE LESSON IS THE PRESCRIPTION

Often in sales, people are more focused on pushing the prospect into what they want them to buy. They think, *what can I get from this prospect when they buy my product/service?* The salesperson is fixated on their own personal gain, not helping the prospect.

What I learned at The Bolt is to reverse that concept and make what you're offering 100% about the client. Prescribe the client what they need to reach their goals and be confident in delivering that result.

When I was first taught this lesson, the best analogy I was ever told was, "Think of yourself as the fitness doctor." When you go to the doctor, they're going to diagnose you. They're going to assess you and prescribe what will cure your illness. The doctor doesn't care about your budget. The doctor doesn't care how you feel about following instructions. The doctor is simply laying out, based on their expertise, what you need to solve your problem. They write the prescription. Then they send you to get your prescription filled from the pharmacy.

The same principle works in fitness. When you view yourself as the expert at what you do and create a plan that solves your prospect's problem, you can prescribe them what they need. They can get help through your prescription of programs or services.

Then the client can pick how they want to move forward. This gives them more ownership and buy-in. It also allows you to ask for higher ticket offers, not just what you think they can afford or are willing to pay. This approach enables you to stay in your genius zone as the expert you truly are.

When I started utilizing prescription-based selling, I went from struggling to sell six-session and twelve-session training packages to selling 100, 200, and 300 sessions at a time.

I could do this because I presented my recommendation as a prescription based on the client's goals and needs. I didn't just use this tactic at The Bolt. I continue to use it today in how I run my businesses and what I teach my coaching clients.

By mastering the process of selling based on prescription instead of dollar amount and getting comfortable asking for the sale, I quickly climbed the ranks. It wasn't long before I was the top producing fitness manager throughout all 24 gym locations, adding millions of dollars to the organization's bottom line.

This experience allowed me to truly understand the sales process from start to finish.

I also learned when you focus on people, the money takes care of itself.

When you combine the earlier principles of being enthusiastic about what you do, adding value, and creating quick wins by prescribing people based on what they want and need instead of what you want in your bank account, you'll find yourself playing the long game and focusing on long-term relationships.

When this is your aim, you will start to succeed and excel. Doing this allowed me to become a top producer at every single one of the companies where I worked. This progression spanned over a decade. It involved learning different processes and systems from people who were comfortable testing what worked and what didn't and finding a combination to bring out the best processes. Next, I would combine everything I'd learned during my mindset evolutions to discover what sales really is.

THE PRINCIPLES

I cover several principles in this section, so make sure you keep reading to get the most out of them.

1. **You'll never truly master anything unless you put in the time**. No course, mastermind, or module will make you Jordan Belfort, Grant Cardone, or any of the other industry titans. Some skills can only be learned by going through the process. Mastering your craft comes from doing the mundane non-sexy tasks on a daily basis. But do that every day, and suddenly, you've put in months of work. Those months add up to years. It's through those years that you will achieve your level of mastery. When you achieve mastery, that's when life gets really good.

2. **Adopt a mindset of, "H**ow *can I be better?"* **Then make sure to review your highlight reel after each sales conversation**. To do this, study the sales you missed more than the ones you earned. As you go over what happened with a lost sale, ask yourself, *what could I have done better?* You have to push yourself. If I'd accepted the fixed mindset from all the companies I've worked with over the span of 10-plus years, I never would've grown. I never would've learned valuable insights to make the one-degree shift of going from bad to good, good to great, and great to excellent. So always keep an open mind no matter where you're at in this process.

3. **Principle number three reminds me of Kobe Bryant because Kobe was obsessed with practice**. His hustle showed up on the court every day. He wasn't focused on the game; he was focused on mastering his craft. As he mastered his craft, it allowed him to excel in the game.

   I make sales a sport. Before, it was about the money. Now, it's like playing a game. To me, sales are just points on a scoreboard. It's not really about the money; it's about doing better today or this month than you did yesterday or last month. Focus on playing hard and practicing these skills. Treat everyone you talk to as if they have an invisible sign saying, *"Make me feel special."* It won't matter if they spend $300 or $5,000 with you. Everyone should be treated exactly the same because that's who you are, and that's the level of integrity you carry.

4. **Gamify the process**. One of the coolest things I had learned working at The Bolt was that they had a monthly trainer sales points system. If you sold a certain amount, you would get a prize. Once I learned this, I was intent on dominating. It also helps that I'm super competitive. I used that drive to push myself to levels I never thought I could reach.

   As you find ways to gamify your sales experience, you can gamify it for your team or your whole company. You can show people how to have fun with the process. Because if people aren't enjoying what they're doing, they won't put in the time to reach the level of mastery that'll actually feel good. If you can lead yourself or your team through a gamified process like the sales points system, you can get the best out of people because you're making it a fun experience. When you focus on running up the points on the scoreboard, everyone wins.

5. **You become the sum of those you hang around with**. I got better because I studied the people who were putting up solid numbers and asked questions of them—regardless of where I worked. I wanted to know what they were doing to succeed, so I would succeed, too. Before long, I rose up the ranks and became one of the people putting up solid numbers.

   Build a relationship with people who are in the same role as you—whether they are working in your company or elsewhere. Find out what they're doing well and right. As you level up and it becomes your turn to give back, make sure you repay the favor to help lift up others who are a bit behind you.

THE BUSINESS APPLICATIONS

You have to constantly sharpen your sword.

1. **It's imperative to commit to either practicing your sales skills on your leads or practicing them with your team**. If you're by yourself, you need to train yourself. If you have a team, you need to train with the team. There's no way around it. You will only get better in sales when you practice what you preach and set what you'd expect. That means you will set time each day or each week to get your practice reps in.

   If you are running the team, do a 15-20-minute sales role-play with your team members every day to get them loosened up as they sharpen their skills. Teach your team a certain aspect of the sales process once a week so they can train, practice, and improve. If you're doing this for yourself, as you check your highlight reel, be honest about what you did well and what needed work. When you're honest, you can break down the areas you need to focus on.

2. Focus on building rapport and asking the right kind of questions to get the information you need to move your prospects and clients along. Work on your presentation and build value and excitement into it. Spend time on your closing—when you ask for the sale—and move your prospective client forward to commit to working with you. Whatever your process is, whatever area you're struggling in, it is critical that you set time to train on it. Only then will you reach your 10,000 hours of mastery.

If you're ready to get on the road to clocking your 10,000 hours, sign up for training and use code GREATNESS247 to get access for FREE here: https://jonathanlautermilch.com/training

CHAPTER 5

MY FIRST ROCK BOTTOM

*"Rock bottom became the solid foundation
on which I rebuilt my life. —JK Rowling"*

Until this point, I've shared stories with you about the challenges I've been through, the victories I've had, and all the lessons in between. Often, to reach heaven in our lives, we have to experience what hell feels like.

During my five-year stint at The Bolt, I became one of the top producers and built a solid team. This was a very small gym tucked away behind a Taco Bell and a liquor store. This gym wasn't supposed to be successful.

The gym did well—which was great, but it wasn't critical for the company because many of the other gyms that were better positioned did most of the heavy lifting. They provided the bulk of the revenue for the organization.

**As I rose to claim to my 15 minutes of fame,
I built the number one producing fitness club
within the organization. But I was actually
forced out of the company by my own team.**

My head wasn't in the right place then because I'd never been that successful before. I'd gotten used to struggling and barely getting by, to having glimmering moments of success. But I'd never truly stood in the spotlight and been recognized by my colleagues and peers. My ego got a hold of me when that happened, and it forced me to realize I wasn't a very good leader.

I did put in the effort by working six and sometimes seven days a week. I drove my team to the standards I expected of them. But the number one failure in my leadership was that I made the successes we achieved about me and not about them.

MY TEAM IS TRYING TO DO WHAT?

It wouldn't be until I heard rumors about how my team was petitioning to have me removed from my management position that I would realize this. Unfortunately, I'd also pissed off my superiors since I'd stopped going to team meetings and started playing by my own rules.

I was under the impression that if you were a producer experiencing success, then you got to make your own rules. That was a wake-up call for me. I learned that's not how corporate America works. So, as I completely pissed off those above me, those beside me, and those below me, I was given an option to move to another location or simply step down and leave the company. After dumping five years of my life into building the company and sacrificing my relationships and health by being so focused on taking care of the business versus myself, I said, "fuck it," and quit.

After I burned my bridges, I had to find a new path. However, within that area, The Bolt was the only real fitness company in town. There weren't a whole lot of other opportunities outside of working for the company. That's when I decided to go out on my own, and I started my first online fitness business.

I thought it would be a piece of cake. I already knew how to sell. I knew how to service. I was the top producer and a young, talented guy with charisma in spades. But, I also knew there was a lot I didn't know or understand when it came to online fitness. So I dumped my entire life savings of $30,000 into business coaches, websites, and damn near every shiny object that promised me the life I so desperately wanted. In retrospect, that fiddling with a bunch of shiny objects over the next couple of years provided me with an expensive lesson. That's because as I opened the doors to my business, I had no idea what was required to be a successful entrepreneur. I didn't realize you need a certain mindset and resilience to make it as an entrepreneur. I didn't realize that the number one skill set you need as a business owner is the ability to market and generate leads. At the time, I had no fucking clue how to do that. At the gym, all the leads had been generated for me.

I was just good at closing and servicing sales with the gym's clients. The stress of building a business I had no clue how to build led to me develop a drinking problem.

I was drinking nearly every day. Anything to take the edge off thinking about my problems.

I was looking for anything to keep me from actually doing the real work. The work on myself, the work by asking the tough questions in the mirror, the boring work that actually leads to success.

As I continued to struggle in the dark, the company that had banished me ironically went out of business less than a year later.

They were acquired by Cobalt's Gym. To say I didn't have the feeling of "I told you so" would be a lie. I had seen the writing on the wall for quite some time. However, because Renée was still with the company, it ended up having a huge impact on me.

She was asked to stay on as they laid off nearly the whole executive team. We were asked to move to the location of their international headquarters: Dallas, Texas.

Once again, corporate found a way to fuck up my plans. Even after I left, and although I was struggling, I was still making enough to be a free man, and that was enough for me at the time.

It was this tough period in our lives that showed Renée and me that we could count on each other. So, I decided to seal the deal and ask her to marry me.

It was the biggest sale I would ever make, even to this day. In late September of 2014, we got married on a Friday and moved halfway across the country the following Monday.

After arriving in Dallas, I once again felt like I was starting all over. Even though I had an online business, I had been making most of my sales through people I knew in person. The move would force me to rely entirely on finding clients online because I knew no one in Dallas.

My income wasn't growing, and our expenses had gone up. I finally hit my endpoint where I had to do one of the hardest things I ever had to do.

I had to suck up my pride and get a job. Sacrificing my ego to make ends meet was one of the hardest choices I ever had to make. In my mind, it meant I was a failure. It meant that I fell short of my expectations. I had also spent every single dime to my name and had less than $1,000. But I had to do what was needed to take care of my family and me.

It was honestly one of the most painful experiences in my life because, in my estimation, I had experienced back-to-back failures. Little did I know these rock bottom moments would teach me some of my most critical life lessons.

If you want to be successful, you must have a compelling reason as to why you are in business for yourself. You need to know why you justify getting up every single day and doing the work. You need to know why you choose to fight the everyday battles an entrepreneur faces.

THE PRINCIPLES

Success can become your biggest threat if you don't check your ego.

In the previous story, there are two main takeaways about my rise to success and eventual downfall. These experiences have left a lasting impression on me and led me to become a better person, leader, and businessman.

1. **Keep your eye on the prize: Winning.** One of the biggest mistakes I made when I let my ego run wild was that I wasn't focused on winning. I was focused on being right. If I had set my mind toward winning, I would have listened to my team. I would have made sure I built them up and told them they were the reason we were successful. I would have expressed to my managers how integral they were to our success. But at the time, I just wanted to be right. In my defense, I was the one producing the results and getting the work done. Still, it really wasn't about me. But because I made it about me, it caused a massive failure that led to years of toxicity in my life.

2. **You will learn a lot more from your failures than you will from your successes**. Getting leadership wrong taught me so much about how to run teams and what leadership is really comprised of. When you keep your eye on winning, which is the result we're all trying to achieve, it doesn't matter whether you're right. Besides, rarely do we have situations that allow us to be right or

wrong. Typically, you can win, or you can be right. But you can't do both. When you're in business for yourself, and your mission is to make sales and grow, no matter what industry you're in, aiming to win always overcomes trying to be right.

APPLICATIONS TO BUSINESS

You can take away four applications from this story and immediately apply them to your business and personal life.

1. **Pay attention to how often you're trying to be right versus trying to win**. This is one of the questions I ask myself every time I'm at odds or at pains with someone I'm trying to influence. Yes, you will run into people who have different opinions and beliefs. It's bound to happen. I recommend surrounding yourself with people who think differently than you. This gives you perspective as you attain your best possible outcome. Don't let your ego get in your way and slip you up. Simply ask yourself, *am I trying to be right, or am I trying to win?*

2. **Keep your eyes on the big picture of what you're trying to do**. Often, you will find when you're faced with challenges, 99% of the time, they don't matter at the end of the day.

   Think about a challenge you're having right now. Now, consider if in a year's time, will it be something you'll even have to think about? Most of the time, you won't need to worry about it. It will dissipate as quickly as it appeared.

Rewire your mind to think of winning. Clearly define what winning is for you and how it contributes to what you're trying to do every single day—with your big picture. Doing this will help you keep your mind wired on the right activity, so you can keep yourself and your team moving in the right direction.

3. **Ask yourself,** *what does winning look like in my life?* Clearly define the areas you really want to work on. Is it your marriage? Is it your relationship with your employees? Is it the relationship with yourself? Or is it your actual business you're trying to grow? What do you define as winning in your business? What is a goal that, if you accomplish it, will lead to winning? When you get clear on the areas that are important to you and define what winning looks like, you can start rewiring your mindset to get more wins.

4. **Sacrifice your pride and ego to get to where you want to go.** Not a day that goes by that I don't wish I could go back to my team and redo what I now know I should have done. When my ego was out of control, I did the best I could, based on who I was and the knowledge I had. I am very grateful for the lessons and missteps I learned from that time because I'm a better leader and person now. But if I could have gone back and let go of my ego and focused

on winning, I could be in a totally different position today. Still, I have to be grateful. Since that happened, I'm here with you, sharing that lesson. Now, fortunately, you won't make the same mistakes that I did.

CHAPTER 6

GET BACK UP; YOU'RE NOT DONE YET

"It's not about how many times you fall, but how many times you get back up." —Abraham Lincoln."

Let me set the stage with this story about three different gym companies that had a profound impact on my development. Working for these three companies enables me to speak to you today.

Re-entering the corporate workforce was the beginning of me eating a big ol' piece of humble pie.

I'd just come from being a free man for the last couple of years. Yes, every day was a struggle, and I was barely getting by, but I was a free man.

GYM #1

I had taken a position—which at the time I thought was beneath me—as a fitness manager for a company called True Force Gym.

True Force Gym was a small mom-and-pop operation with four locations that were all run by a husband and wife team. I thought working there would be a close second to being an entrepreneur since I was working for a fellow entrepreneur. I hoped the owners would give me more autonomy and freedom within my position.

As I started to build relationships with the team, I damn sure knew I wouldn't make the same mistakes in leadership I'd made last time. So, I made getting to know each team member on a personal level my absolute goal as I devised a plan for how to get them to work as a team.

As I asked the team what they needed to be successful, they all responded with, "We need better systems," as all their systems and client acquisition strategies were really outdated. They were still flyering parking lots and cold-calling people! They were also still relying on asking members on the gym floor if they wanted to go through a personal training consultation. All those strategies work, but they're not nearly as efficient as they could be. Especially since the trainers worked on a draw system. In a draw system, every moment spent not training clients comes out of the trainers' commissions.

When I observed this about their business, I knew the lessons I learned spending $30,000 to become an online entrepreneur would come in handy. This gym had leads; they just needed a *funnel* to convert them into sales.

So, I started implementing different systems and strategies that not only helped the gym increase the number of new clients and members we brought in but also scaled my team's time tremendously. Within 60 days of deploying one of my marketing campaigns, we added 40 new clients in the first 30 days. This provided more financial stability for the trainers, which led to a greater opportunity for the company to build its backend revenue.

This story illustrates that even today and especially in smaller gyms, there are a lot of systems—that are not being utilized—that can dramatically improve a fitness business's results.

After my success as a fitness manager, I got my first promotion to general manager and was assigned to run one of the company's struggling locations.

It was honestly worse than an episode of *Bar Rescue*. The staff had zero accountability, there were zero systems in place, and the members treated the gym like it was their personal trash can.

Most of the time, I found myself playing mediator between staff members who had toxic relationships with one another—which is not what I was built to do.

I knew this wasn't in alignment with my purpose and skillset, but I wanted to make sure I left the gym better than I found it.

So, I staffed it with the right team members, trained them, and then decided to accept an opportunity as a fitness director for another company.

GYM #2

That company was Perfect 10 Fitness Center or P10 for short. P10 supplied subcontracted personal trainers to a large gym chain. They were solely responsible for the personal training revenue and services within each gym. I ran the sales team, which worked independently from the service team. The service team was made up of personal trainers whose only job was to train clients;

they didn't make any of the sales. The interesting thing about this business model was that all the personal trainers were subcontractors and not employees. This changed the dynamic of how we worked together. There's a big difference between how an employer can manage employees versus how they can manage contractors.

I liked this opportunity because my main goal was to drive sales, and my main driver at the time was to make a solid living for my wife.

As I worked with this company, I found out they were struggling to get their sales numbers up. They had run into the same problems that True Force Gym had due to their marketing and sales strategies. P10 was also using outdated, passive strategies to acquire appointments and convert prospects into clients. So, I deployed the same campaign I had used at True Force Gym but, it wouldn't come without its challenges.

For starters, I had to battle with toxic sales reps. One even tried to pick a fistfight with me in the parking lot. Of course, I fired him.

Then some trainers were sleeping with their clients, and they had to be reprimanded.

And I had a broken relationship to mend between P10 and the actual gym staff. I was spending two hours a day just commuting to this location, where I would spend ten hours a day, six days a week.

My work was more than cut out for me.

But once I could get a few tactics in place, within the first six months, we generated $10,000 in new recurring revenue.

Sure, I had fine-tuned the process for signing up new clients, but we were losing them just as fast as we were getting them. This was because of the subpar service standards that had been set for the subcontracted trainers. Imagine trying to sail across the sea, but your boat has a bunch of holes in it, so it's always taking on water. You can imagine the frustration I had from putting in the time and effort required to bring in new clients, only to see them leave within a matter of months after working with their trainer.

If we were going to be successful, I had to develop a culture with standards that both sides of the team could buy into. We also had to learn to work together as one unified team. I started to bring trainers into the sales training and the sales team into the service training. I focused on those who could bridge the gap between service and sales.

When it comes to fitness, sales is critical because clients don't get the results they're after unless the sale is made. But if we're not providing a great service, then the sale doesn't matter because the client didn't get results.

After I united the team, got them focused on the same mission, and made sure everyone was paid appropriately for their role in that mission, we truly started to grow.

We also no longer focused on price selling as it was destroying our margins and creating a buying culture around running specials. So I focused on raising the value of what we were offering and refused to present lower price packages. This led to fewer sales but, our average value per client went up dramatically so we could accomplish more with fewer clients. It also led to higher quality clients as I could vet them during the sales process.

It would take nearly a year, but we were consistently drafting $10-12k more per month than the team had before I got there. However, during that time, they had a leadership change. I had really enjoyed working for my first boss, which was a rare experience for me because I hated being told what to do back then. When he exited the company, new leadership came in.

Let's just say this new guy and I were not on the same page. When I saw how the company culture was about to shift for the worst, I started looking for another opportunity—which leads us to the third and final story in this chapter. The gym I landed at after P10 had the most profound impact on me of any other experience I'd had because it was where all the pieces came together.

GYM #3

I moved on from P10 to take a fitness manager position with a place I'll call *Always Open Fitness & Health*. It's one of the largest fitness organizations on the planet. When I interviewed for the position, I met with the general manager and sales manager, who showed me around the facility. For the first time, I went into an interview with a consultant mindset instead of a prospective employee mindset. This was because I was more concerned with making sure I knew what I was getting myself into than landing a job.

By then, I was so sick and tired of being subject to the bait and switch when I interviewed for a position. I was done with being told how well a company or club was doing or how great the team was, just to get in there and realize everything was a complete shit show. Just so you know, if someone starts a sentence with, "Historically speaking," it means the location you're about to take over is tanking and tanking hard.

The truth is: *"It's going to take a complete overhaul and a lot of my time to turn this shit in the right direction."* But as I started asking questions about the business and their culture, for the first time ever, the general manager gave me the most honest answers I'd ever heard. She shot me straight, and it's what closed me on accepting the offer. They were only doing about one thousand dollars a month in training and only had two trainers. They were doing well selling memberships, but couldn't sell training at point-of-sale to save their lives. I saw the opportunity to build that up and gladly accepted the position of fitness manager, knowing it was going to be up to me and no one else to build what they needed.

Immediately, I applied the same tactics and strategies I'd used at the last company. We started generating clientele through the new members coming into the facility, which allowed me to bring on more training staff. I had access to every gym lead, and I was hungry.

In my mind, each lead already had the money for training. I just had to ask for it.

I recruited great trainers I'd worked with at the previous two companies to help me build the club. It was a great arrangement for them because I would hand feed them clients and help them reach their personal goals. Soon, we had a small team of four trainers. My mindset this go-around was to build a team of Spartans—meaning, fewer trainers, but those on the team would be the best of the best. By keeping the team tight, spending my time developing them, and making sure I was the top producer, the gym increased its training revenue from $1,000 a month to $36,000 with only four trainers! The lesson I learned through this process was that you don't need to have a lot of people on your team; you just need to have the right ones. You need the ones who see your vision and who buy into it.

As I built the team, I realized that what I was building wasn't a team. It was a family. I'll never forget my trainer, Jesse, who I convinced to follow me there in exchange for me helping him build his business to the point where he could afford to move out of his parents' house. He now owns and operates his own training business and is a client of mine. I'll never forget how one of our trainers, Zeia, was moving and had no one to help her. So, we banded together as a team and helped her move into her new apartment. Because they showed up for me, I made sure I showed up for them—in every area of their lives. Everyone on that team went on to become leaders. Developing people became my second greatest addiction to making sales.

As I groomed them into who I believed they could become and who they wanted to become, I didn't realize I had become their "work dad." This was one of the proudest moments of my life. Several of those trainers now work for my companies, Fit Pro Collective and Smart Shark. We're on a mission to help fit pros get what they're worth.

But all great things must come to an end when you don't control the land. Eventually, the story I've seen played out in every big box fitness company I've worked for came to fruition when the company decided to massively overhaul its upper management. Not surprisingly, this led to a trickle-down effect. Suddenly, commitments and promises that leadership had made me were denied. I was told an agreement I had made with upper management to increase the compensation tier of my location if we hit $50,000 a month in revenue would not be honored.

That was when I learned the lesson: you can't build a kingdom on sand.

If you're trying to build your kingdom on a wavering foundation, in this case, a company you don't own, you won't control all the variables. *You aren't in control.* Whatever you have been building can be swept out from under you in an instant.

Despite my difficulties with the new management, this job was one more notch in my belt. It gave me the proof I needed to be convinced that I had what it took to create whatever I wanted. But I had to own it. And it all started with having what I felt I was worth taken away from me. It helped me realize what I was great at and what I was truly worth. Now it was time for me to figure out how to put the skills together that I had developed to create something bigger than myself.

THE PRINCIPLE

I have just one lesson to share with you in this chapter

1. **You'll never lose until you quit**. As long as you don't quit, you will never fail. As long as you always get back up, you will always have another opportunity to regain what you lost.

   After failing in my attempt to climb the corporate ladder, then failing to become a successful online entrepreneur, I had to pick myself up. I had to go through the lessons that running fitness teams for multiple companies taught me.

They all served as a whetstone for sharpening my skills. They each groomed me for the life I have now, and that's what being groomed for greatness is all about. The tricky thing is, we don't see the lessons we're learning in the moment. We just think, *why is this happening to me?*

When you're in the middle of trying to figure out what to do and how to save your job, you question all your decisions and thoughts. Your self-limiting beliefs kick in. That's understandable. But if you take a step back and see what you're going through honestly, you'll understand how it will benefit you. If I hadn't gone through the experience of leading teams for those different companies and not had the failures I did, it wouldn't have led me to today—to me speaking to you through this book. I couldn't have gone on to help hundreds of fitness professionals around the world live a life built around getting what they're worth in every area of their lives. So, if you adopt one thing from this chapter, let it be this: When you make up your mind to never quit, that's the exact moment you'll set yourself up to win.

THE BUSINESS APPLICATIONS

You can apply these three applications to your business today:

1. **Don't discard what seems like a failure**. You will often make mistakes in business. You're actually more likely to make mistakes than you are to achieve success. The best part about being in business is you can get it wrong ten times, but you only have to get it right once to earn a massive payoff.

Your failures work as a stepping stone that leads you to finally getting it right. So be grateful for your failures. They're taking you in the direction that you need to grow.

2. **All your successes and failures have led you to where you are today and will lead you to where you want to go tomorrow.**

Really reflect on the journey you've been on, whether that's in the fitness industry or another industry. Maybe you want to reflect on something that happened in your personal life. Whatever it is, take a moment and think about how those events connect with one another. You'll start to see a theme as you relive each one. Once you find the themes, it's easier to see the direction you're moving in.

When you know where you're going and that there's a purpose behind everything you've gone through, you can be grateful for everything that happens. It won't matter, whether it's good or bad.

3. **As you're going through a painful experience, whether past or present, try to see the puzzle pieces.** Understand how those pieces fit into the story of your life and who you're meant to be.

Every single company I've worked for represents one puzzle piece in my story. I've worked for over eight different companies throughout four states. In my experience with each company, I acquired a puzzle piece I needed to create what I call "my masterpiece." This masterpiece is the wisdom I have gained. It's part of what we share in our Fit Pro Collective Program to take the guesswork out of being a successful fit pro. We help trainers, so they don't have to go through the same struggles we did.

As you reflect on your life and think about your own puzzle pieces, just know that each piece is designed for you on purpose. That's where the idea of being groomed for greatness comes from. Each lesson is part of the grooming process; it is one more piece that will complete the puzzle of your life. When you put them all together, you'll understand what you were put on this earth to do.

If you're looking for additional resources to help you get what you're worth, visit: https://jonathanlautermilch.com/resources

CHAPTER 7

THE BIRTH OF GETTING
WHAT YOU'RE WORTH

"If you know your worth then go get what you're worth.
But you gotta be willing to take the hits and not point
fingers saying you ain't where you wanna
be because of him or her or anybody."
—Rocky Balboa

By now, you've heard about lessons, stories, and principles based on the idea that you are constantly being groomed for greatness.

**One lesson that helped me reach this realization
is learning that you're told what you're worth
or you're demonstrating what you're worth
to the world around you.**

This is relevant in all areas of your life.

YOU HAVE TO ASK FOR IT!

No one is just going to give you what you're worth because you are a nice person. Whether you work for a person or company, they will always try to find a way to get you to work for them for the lowest fee or wage possible. The same goes for your personal relationships. It's in our human nature. Until you grab the reins and take control of your destiny, you won't be able to proclaim what your true value is in business and life.

This lesson has been echoed over and over to me through a culmination of life experiences. As I already shared with you, I've worked for eight companies in four states, and I've reached the same outcome with every single one of them. Ironically enough, on paper, I look like I can't keep a job. This is because I was looking for my worth in others instead of doing the work and discovering it within myself. After trial and error, I discovered that working for these companies was never going to allow me to meet the level of expectations and aspirations I had for myself. This is what sparked the movement behind "getting what you're worth." It all begins with the value you see in yourself.

THE CATALYST

The last fitness company I worked at was the final straw for me. It was the catalyst for drastically changing my life. Later, I would see that it was my biggest blessing in disguise.

I had taken a role as a fitness manager for a small chain of fitness clubs in Texas and was running one of their newer locations that had been struggling for the past year. They were awesome at bringing in new members but had a tough time growing the personal training team and revenue to the level they had expected. This was a brand new club, and they weren't hitting their numbers. I had to rebuild the whole team from scratch. The team in place wasn't being held accountable, they weren't being developed, and they had zero resources detailing the running of a successful training business. My plate was definitely full.

On top of that, I was fighting a battle on two fronts. One on the front lines with the staff and one with the executive team who constantly micromanaged every decision and move I made. They not only wanted to win, but they wanted to be right about how we won, even though the way they had been doing things was exactly how they ended up where they were, with poor results and a high staff turnover.

Now, if this is what would have been communicated when I had accepted the job offer, I would have been okay with it. But I was promised autonomy over my team, that I could run things as I saw fit because they had hired me to get the result. Once again, I had been baited and switched into a position. My resentment toward this tired business model and "leadership style" grew to new heights. Yet, as I continued to work with the company, I quickly found out the reason why the executive team was operating this way. The CEO was breathing down all the executive teams' necks to get them to produce the results he wanted. It even got to the point where the CEO started contacting gym-level managers directly to micromanage them.

I remember getting phone calls at eight and nine o'clock on Friday nights directly from the CEO. He would ask me, *"What are you going to do to make sure we hit numbers the next day?"* The incredible thing was that these calls would come right after the team and I *had* produced great numbers the month before, hitting our goals. It was the typical leadership approach of drilling your producers to make up for those who aren't producing. If you want to drive your top talent away, trust me, that is the way to do it.

Before becoming the top producing fitness manager for the quarter, it seemed like nothing I did was ever enough. I was extremely frustrated. I was extremely stressed. The time I was putting in versus the money I was receiving made it obvious that what I was doing wasn't worth it. Still, that experience of feeling so much pressure to get a result and having it all thrown onto my shoulders, with little to no support, did something for me. It created an "aha" moment which revealed that if I was going to work this hard and this long to get these types of results, I might as well be doing it for myself. Once that realization hit, I started plotting my exit strategy. I examined what it was that I really wanted to do, which was to coach, develop trainers, and work with gym owners to show them that there was a better and more sustainable way to grow without burning their staff out in the process.

This was the beginning of what you know today as Smart Shark. But it all began by working for a toxic company with unrealistic standards that pushed me to my breaking point. This led to my evolution. I realized I could put the same intensity and effort into building something that was mine versus building it for someone else who never appreciated who I was and the value I brought to the team.

> **It was also my first epiphany that if you want to get paid what you're worth, you've got to go get what you're worth.**

Getting what you're worth starts with your mindset, it starts with the belief in yourself, and it starts with the realization that life is going to be hard.

It's going to take time. So you might as well put the time you have toward what you want to build for yourself, whether that's a legacy, a great impact, or financial stability for you and your family. Maybe you want to build a kingdom to bless each and every person you come in contact with. No matter what your motivation is, you are simply one mindset shift away from being able to go out and get what you're worth.

THE PRINCIPLE

1. **You can either be told what you're worth, or you can go out and get what you know you're worth**. Every time we go out into the world, we constantly have to battle with people over our values and our work. It doesn't matter if you're an employee, are working in an organization, or are out in the sales field talking to prospects and trying to communicate and convey the value you offer through your solution. The sooner you realize your worth is not based on other people's opinions of you but that it comes from your decisions, your true worth will sink in.

All the pain I went through over the five-year period when I had to eat humble pie by going back into the workforce allowed me to check my ego and focus on mastering my craft. If you want to lead, you must learn how to follow first.

There are two main lessons in this chapter. The first is to realize that you determine your worth. The second is that every single experience you have leading up to making the decision of what you're worth is exactly what being groomed for greatness is all about.

THE BUSINESS APPLICATIONS

You can take away several applications from this chapter and apply them immediately to your life and business.

1. **Life is going to kick your ass every opportunity it gets**. But the lessons and experiences through those ass-kickings are what mold you into who you are supposed to be. When we understand that life happens for us, not to us, we can talk and think from a place of gratitude when we're going through the ass-kicking that life delivers to us. That one mindset shift can make you a lot of money and put you on a different trajectory in life.

2. **You always have a choice**. I could've stayed where I was and continued to get the same results over and over and over again. I could've tried to change how business was done to make things better as I worked within the organization. But eventually, I realized I couldn't change the

system from the inside. Instead, I had to create something, so I could influence that change from the outside. We all have the ability to make choices in our businesses and lives. Remind yourself that no matter your situation, you always have a choice as to what you want to do.

3. Whatever you want to call that thing up above: God the Universe, Yahweh, aliens, a Higher Power, it doesn't matter. **The entity will tell you throughout your life, "Here's the lesson." The people who don't lean into the lesson and apply it to their lives will end up endlessly repeating the same lesson.**

Many times, a test disguised as a challenge is thrown in our path with opportunity on the other side of it, but we don't realize the test is designed to teach us a lesson that will lead us to the opportunity. So, we miss out. The danger is that when we don't understand the lesson, we will repeat the same mistakes over and over again. All of a sudden, we've lived the same year for ten years straight. Our lives become like *Groundhog Day*. Take a second to step back, be honest, and say, "Here's what's happening to me. These are the results I'm getting. And they aren't the results I want. I've tried every possible way to get a better result, and it hasn't happened. So, what's the lesson in it? What is it that I need to change, that I need to know in order to grow, so I can get better results?"

When you focus on the lessons, passing the test becomes extremely easy over time.

CHAPTER 8

CUTTING THE PATH TO FREEDOM

"Don't follow the path. Blaze the trail."
—*Jordan Belfort*

As I took my second stab at becoming a successful entrepreneur, I realized that I had to go about starting my new business differently than my first.

I DIDN'T KNOW WHAT I DIDN'T KNOW

When I launched my first business, I didn't know about the skills I needed to develop to be successful.

The second time around, I used my years of experience mastering my craft to put together a plan. If I was going to create a path to freedom for my family, myself, and all of my fellow Fit Pros around the world, I needed to change up my plan.

I was working at a company called the Lone Star State Fitness Center when the idea for my second company hit me. As I set out building it, I realized that I had to figure out how to take care of day-to-day needs, like our mortgage and bills, as I constructed my future.

I had to take care of today, so I could build tomorrow.

I also realized that I needed to put myself in a position that would permit me enough time to dedicate to building my new business. I followed one of my previous lessons of eating humble pie and being grateful for it when I took a part-time job as a personal trainer working for a fellow fitness manager I had met at Always Open Health & Fitness. This gave me the flexibility I needed to get my business off the ground.

When I was hired at Always Open Health & Fitness, I wasn't a fan of my new manager. It helped that I knew him and that he knew I was great at what I did. When he gave me an opportunity to work part-time, I could make ends meet. I humbled myself and took a step back to become a personal trainer. I didn't run the gym. I no longer called the shots. I wasn't a "leader" within the organization.

My mindset was to report to work and do what I had to do to take care of the bills. Then when I was done training clients, I could dedicate my time to building what would become Smart Shark. During this transition, I had all the fun conversations that a husband and wife have when you're making such a huge life change. With my previous track record of failing in my first business and constantly hopping around between companies, the trust with my wife wasn't exactly stellar.

That didn't matter. I knew something had to change, and she knew something had to change with me as well. If it didn't, we would continue the cycle of me being openly depressed and miserable. So, Renée reluctantly agreed and got on board. She helped me support and build my company, Smart Shark. But it all start-ed with me proving to her through my actions that I was com-mitted to doing the work. I had to prove my commitment by humbling myself and taking a job I didn't want to take. I not only had to do the work to build up a client base at the gym, but I also had to do the work outside of that to build my business. That meant working seven days a week, even when I least felt like it, because I was hungry for where I wanted to be.

**As I look back on the lessons I've shared with you,
I can't tell you how many times I had to ask myself
as I was getting started again,
*do you want to be right, or do you want to win?***

I had gotten to the point where there was no more ego. Life had beaten it out of me. I was obsessed with finding a way to win, and I was damn sure determined to find a way to do it.

WHAT'S YOUR FREEDOM NUMBER?

As I was building, I set goals for myself. My first goal was iden-tifying what my freedom number was that I needed to hit so I could justify quitting my job. I had to create that security and consistency to make sure Renée was okay.

At the time, the number was pretty low. It was only about $4,000 a month. I like to think I'm a complicated man with simple needs, so I tend to spend on what I need in life and no more. This char-acteristic worked well for me as I found a way to drastically get rid of everything that wasn't serving me. When I did this, I got clear on what my freedom number was. Then I set a target to meet it within six months. But I was able to do it in four. The transition was easier than I thought since it made no sense to keep my job after hitting my freedom number.

When I quit that part-time job, not only was my income way higher, but it required a fraction of the amount of time because I was no longer selling my time for dollars. I was getting our client's results, and that's what matters. It was time to quit anyway since I was running out of time to spend on my business. We had massively increased our business, and because of that, I was losing more of my free time. It became a no-brainer to go all-in before I spread myself too thin. Going from a side hustle to solopreneur brought with it what you might have heard: With new levels come new devils. This means that as you continue to level up in your business and life, you attract different problems.

I'M FREE!

Going from working for a company I was miserable at to being "free" with more complex and challenging problems brought out such gratitude in me. I was so grateful that I had the problems I did. They far outweighed the pain I'd dealt with when I was living a lifestyle and working at a job I was no longer fulfilled with. Gratitude for my problems would be a recurring experience as I kept leveling up in my entrepreneurial journey.

In the first year of running your own business, you will focus on getting things off the ground, getting clear on the clients you serve, your value proposition, and knowing all the challenges that a startup business goes through. I went through those very same challenges.

I replaced the minimum income of what I needed to provide for my family. It wasn't much, but I was liberated! As we entered the second year in business, the work I had been putting in for over a year was starting to bear fruit. I was beginning to become the go-to guy for helping fit pros get their businesses off the ground, and we had developed a solid track record of doing so.

New Levels, New Devils

Then, one of the best and worst things to ever happen—happened.

When COVID-19 hit, it demolished the fitness industry and how it used to operate.

COVID-19 had a negative impact on many people's businesses and lives. My heart truly goes out to everyone affected. For many of those who pivoted and followed the opportunity to go online, their choice became a huge launchpad to experience a different level of fulfillment and success. Before COVID-19 hit, we had already been helping personal trainers and gym owners transition to move some aspects of their businesses online. We were in the right place at the right time with the right solution.

COVID-19 was the tidal wave that moved Smart Shark to the next level. It was the biggest blessing and curse. It accelerated our growth, and I was grateful for that. But it also caused me to feel such sorrow for the people who were struggling.

I saw how many coaches were scared to death, and as a result, I opened up the doors and offered the entire training I had been doing with our clients for free.

I knew what it felt like to be in that place, and if I could do anything to help, I damn sure was going to do it. From that free course, we hit a new level. Many of the coaches who went through the training decided to hire us to help them transition online.

Yet again, this would be another experience with "new levels, new devils."

Through that experience and growth, Smart Shark was no longer just about me. I had to bring on a team to help service all our new clients. This was when I moved from being a solopreneur to an entrepreneur. I now have a team of people who build our funnels and websites. I have a team of people who handle customer service. I have a team of people who write sales copy. I have a team of people who do tech support. I even partnered with another coach who coaches our clients. Bringing on all these critical roles put me back into the leadership seat. Business became about supporting the team members I'd brought on.

IT ALL COMES TO A HEAD

All the lessons I've learned through the years of running gyms, the mistakes I've made, and the times that I got it right finally came to a head. I was able to apply the lessons and principles I learned to grow a digital team full of team members across the world.

Growing has been one of the best experiences. I went from struggling to hit our monthly goal to operating at a set level of abundance. We get to provide for other team members and their families. That trickle-down effect and the impact it has on their networks has led to us serving over 100 fit pros across the world. Our impact resonates through the businesses I own, but it all started with the guy who got sick and tired of being sick and tired. The guy who decided he wanted to make a change. The guy who realized he simply had to start putting in the work. It started with a side hustle that became a full-blown company.

Often, we overestimate what we can do in a month but vastly underestimate what we can do in a year. Imagine what you could do in a year if you got focused on what you want.

THE PRINCIPLE

1. **There will be short-term tasks you have to accomplish today to take care of your business, and there will be long-term power moves you need to execute**. Of course, there will be things you need to do to build for tomorrow, too. When you reach higher levels in your business that require you to make different types of decisions, you'll experience new kinds of problems. The challenges you face in your side hustle will be different than the challenges you face when you're running your business full-time. Meeting the challenges you face while running a side hustle will help you level up your skills so you can transition to becoming a full-time solopreneur.

   At some point, after reaching the milestone of building your team, you'll become the CEO of your organization. At this level, the same concept applies.

   You still need to ask yourself: *What are the activities I need to focus on right now? Then ask yourself: What are the long-term power moves I have to make that will help me continue to build and grow my company in the direction I'm trying to take it?* Getting extremely clear on those answers is going to make life and business simple. It will allow you to take meaningful action. No matter what, success is all about taking action.

THE BUSINESS APPLICATIONS

Let me leave you with two simple applications that are relevant to your business.

1. I had to learn the first business application as I transitioned into running a successful second startup. **The business application is: What has to get done today to keep the business going**? What are the behaviors? What are the power moves that will help you build for the future?

   While money isn't everything, it's up there. So when you are thinking about what you need to get done today, think about the money. Make sure you keep your thumb on the pulse of the money you have coming in and out of the business. And whether you're starting off as a side hustle, working as a solopreneur, or are leading an entire team, you will need to be aware of certain behaviors and tasks that will take care of the business today—and every day.

2. **When I was leveling up, I learned that the duties and responsibilities I needed to perform as a solopreneur wouldn't work on my new level.** In this stage, I came into contact with a concept known as "the power move" versus "the forced move."

   A power move takes longer to get results from. It creates long-term branding and a long-term benefit for you and the marketplace. A power move might be starting a podcast, writing a book, or recording weekly videos that educate and entertain your audience. Power moves involve doing what may not take care of your business's needs today, but with consistency, you'll see changes over the next 60-90 days. After that, you'll see those changes at six months and again at 12 months. You'll recognize what you are doing will compound massively over time.

Once you're a full-time solopreneur or a leader of a team, you'll want to get clear on what the power moves are for you. Then, you'll want to dedicate enough time to focus on consistently executing them.

Remember, forced moves—the tasks you need to do daily to sustain your business combined with power moves— the actions that make running your business easier over time, position you to grow your company to levels you never imagined.

CHAPTER 9

MONEY IS JUST THE SCORE OF IMPACT

"Money is just the score of impact."
—Jeff Dousharm"

As you go through life, you're going to experience new levels and standards you choose to live by. It's part of what makes this thing called life worth living.

When you're first starting out, everything seems to revolve around money.

Do I have enough?

How do I get more?

How come that guy over there seems to have so much of it while I have so little?

The truth is, your income is directly influenced by how you think about money.

I want to share with you one of the biggest money mindset shifts I've experienced. If you choose to adopt it, it will serve you well.

That mindset shift is this: Money is just the score of impact.

Let me explain.

THE CHANGING DEFINITIONS OF MONEY

When I started out in the industry over 13 years ago, money was everything. I didn't have a lot of it. To me, money meant being able to live independently. Money meant being able to do what I wanted when I wanted. Money meant being able to buy the toys I wanted so I could experience life how I desired.

Now, I've realized I don't need that much, nor do I care about "things." What's important to me is the impact that I can have on other people's lives and the lifestyle I get to live. When I started to realize these truths, sales became dramatically easier for me. What I was doing wasn't about the money anymore. It was about solving someone else's problems and seeing the effect that had in every area of their life.

If money is constantly on your mind and stressing you out, ask yourself this: *what do I need to earn to live the life I want to live*?

In other words, how much do you need to make?

What is your freedom number? How much do you need to earn to get to the point where money no longer stresses you out? Until you know that number and until you reach that goal, whatever that number is, you're going to feel like you're on a hamster wheel. You're going to feel like you're Bill Murray in *Groundhog Day*. If you haven't seen the movie, his character repeats the same day over and over again no matter what he does differently. Break free from that cycle, and you'll get unstuck. Once you do, you'll be able to work toward generating the income you need to live the lifestyle you want.

WHAT DOES IT ALL MEAN TO YOU?

Reach that point where you don't really need more money, and you'll have entered the phase where what you earn is just abundance. Then you've got to find out what will fulfill you long-term. You'll need to understand what your impact on this earth is. What can you do better than anyone out there? You'll want to ask yourself these questions: *What impact am I having? What problems am I solving? What challenges am I helping people solve?*

I learned how to find these answers through a personal development leader. Bob Proctor conducted a training called the Mission in Commission.

He taught that when you truly understand why you're focused on a mission, commitment becomes a byproduct.

You can apply this analogy to a client working out in the gym, too. If they're so focused on losing weight that they're constantly getting on and off the scale every day, they're focusing on the wrong target. The people who are successful in the gym concentrate on the right behaviors and the right attitude. They show up daily and are excited about what they're doing. With each day, they get another chance to better themselves. Through that mindset, weight loss becomes a byproduct.

The same concept applies to sales and growing a business. If you get really obsessed and clear about who you want to help, and you help them better than anyone else, money becomes the byproduct of your service. When you find your freedom number and shift your mindset about money, you can stop focusing on your money and start focusing on your mission. And when you become obsessed with your mission, financial success is likely to follow.

When you focus on money, you make bad decisions.

When you focus on money, you don't keep your clients' best interests at heart.

When you have a broke money mindset, other people can feel it, sense it, and see it.

But when you truly want to help and serve people, and you're confident in asking for what you and your service are worth, sales becomes just another part of your day.

Don't forget; abundance starts with understanding this principle: Money is just the score of your impact. It's the number on the scoreboard and in your business.

THE PRINCIPLES

This chapter contains three principles that you can apply immediately to your business. Maybe you've noticed a theme here, but I want to make these principles simple and applicable.

1. **If you help people by actually helping them first, you make this weird thing called money**. Most people are wired to think that they have to sell someone first and help them second. But the basis of a relationship's success is value. If you add value first by doing what you can to solve someone's problem, and if you're intent on building the relationship, money becomes part of the process.

   Think about what it's like to date and find your dream man or dream woman. Naturally, you will build the relationship first by going on dates.

   When you spend time together, commitment is formed. The same truth applies to sales. Ask yourself, what problem can I solve and what value can I provide upfront, so it becomes a no-brainer to want to do business with me?

2. Principle number two is based on what I've built my business around. It's something we're taught to unlearn—especially in the fitness industry—when we're told we need to sell first and help people second. It's this: **Fitness has an impact**. I haven't met a single fitness professional who told me the reason they got into this industry was that they wanted to be filthy rich. They always tell me they got into this industry because fitness had an impact on their life. Fitness had an impact on their family's life. Fitness had an impact on someone they knew. It was the desire to want to impact the lives of others that inspired them to be in this business in the first place.

When you give yourself permission to provide value up-front by helping people first, they will want to work with you. You will have established yourself as someone who they know, like, and most importantly, trust.

3. **You don't need fancy sales techniques like upselling and downselling funnels, this type of sales flow, or that kind of sales flow.** People don't want to be sold, but they love to buy. If you don't believe me, check out an electronic store during Black Friday. You'll see tons of people spending money on what they want. Very rarely do we see that many people spend money on what they need.

Focus on building the value of what you do by getting people to actually want what you do. Then they will want to work with you. If you can make fitness fun and get results, people will line up outside your door wanting to work with you and your team. So, ask yourself this question if you're ever unsure about how to proceed in your business: *Who can I help today?* Then chase the people you can help. I promise you, the money will take care of itself.

THE BUSINESS APPLICATIONS

There are a few applications I want to share with you that relate to a specific mindset shift. I had to realize if I was going to lead people who sell fitness, I had to find a way to inspire them first. Then I could compensate them well enough for them to justify working in fitness as a lifelong career.

1. **Establish KPIs—key performance indicators.** We need to know what to measure that will lead to business growth. If we don't inspect what we expect, we won't know where we're going. It's just like working with a fitness client. If we're not doing monthly reassessments, how will we know the program's working? And *we* need to know this because if the program's not working, we have to make adjustments to get back on track. It's no different for your business.

   The KPIs I've built within my organizations have always been based on the right behaviors. What are the behaviors you need to engage in to achieve success?

   If you want to grow active clients, you need to know the right KPIs to measure. For example, you must know the number of people who are interested in hearing about your service and how you can help them. When you know this, then you can set appointments.

   When I was running teams, I would get my team members obsessed with leads and appointments. That's because I knew, worst-case scenario, as long as we had enough leads and appointments, we would find success, even if my people were terrible at sales. Over time, I would work with them on developing the skills they needed to get better at sales. But if we hadn't been tracking the right behaviors and there were no prospects to talk to, there would have been no reason to develop sales skills.

2. **Once you get your KPIs in order, continue to focus on the right behaviors**. The last thing you want to do is stress out yourself or your team about things they can't directly control. For example, let's say you're the leader of a fitness team and you're talking to one of your team members, Bob. The last thing you want to say to Bob is, "You need to hit X amount of dollars this month, or we're going to have to do a performance improvement plan." This is another way of saying, "I'm going to walk you just a little bit further out the door."

Instead, try saying something like, "Hey, Bob, you need to focus on having X number of conversations with prospects per day." If you do this, sales will take care of itself because Bob will be focused on providing value to the prospects, which is something he can control. If we get Bob focused on conveying the value of what you and your team provide, and he focuses on consistently demonstrating value to enough people, Bob will make sales.

As Bob makes sales, his profits will increase. As Bob's profits increase, Bob will continue to make more and more sales. When you get your team to focus on the right behaviors and monitor their KPIs, you will motivate them to attain the results you all want. When they experience wins, they'll believe in themselves even more than they did before. Then they'll become excited about what they are doing, which leads to self-motivation.

Thank you so much for reading this book. As soon as you close it, you can immediately apply the strategies learned here to your business and start reaping the benefits NOW. That's how my courses are designed as well.

When you're ready to start playing big and expand your greatness, click on the link below and use the code GREATNESS247 to get access for FREE:

https://jonathanlautermilch.com/training.

I can't wait to hear from you and help you finally get what you're worth!

CHAPTER 10

CONCLUSION

"Intellectual growth should commence at birth and cease only at death." —Albert Einstein

Throughout life, we get a handful of moments that truly define us. It's what we choose to do in those moments that determine where we end up.

I'm far from being done, but I'm damn grateful for where I'm at, and it's due to the nine defining moments of my life that I shared with you in the previous chapters of this book.

Learning the value of developing a strong will at a very young age set the tone for my life. When you strengthen your desire to win, you'll always find the right opportunities.

Understanding that we are built to influence and persuade others to make good choices is what gave me permission to lean into sales, which has helped me change a lot of lives.

Knowing that life specifically designs our struggles to bring out the best in us has made me look forward to challenges and setbacks. All because I now know that what I want is just on the other side.

Developing relentless discipline around honing my craft is what allowed me to become one of the best at what I do. We become what we consistently work toward.

Accept that there will be setbacks along the way and that they're just part of your journey, and know that who you become in the process of clarifying and accomplishing your mission is far more important than any result you'll ever achieve.

Realize that your value doesn't come from others but from what you see and develop within yourself. Everyone has a super-power. You just have to give yourself permission to use it, serve others, and ask for what you want in return.

Learn about the levels you have to go through in business to focus on the type of work you should be doing based on your current level. This will allow you to be grateful for where you are but hungry for where you want to go.

And finally, evolve from seeing money as a thing we must have to seeing money as a resource to use. Know that everything you need is already around you.

Embracing an abundant mindset and focusing on the behaviors that create income instead of focusing on the income itself will help you lead a less stressful and more fulfilling life.

I truly hope this book has given you value and insights on how you can go get what you're worth. Everything you've gone through up until this point has been specifically designed for you and you alone.

Your challenges have been set up to groom you for who you're supposed to become. The world needs the most elite version of you so you can be a light that inspires the people you were built to serve.

Embrace the good and embrace the bad. It's the combination of those that will lead you to your destiny.

Now, go get what you're worth because you deserve to win.

ACKNOWLEDGMENTS

There have been tons of people who have helped bring this book to fruition that I would like to thank.

Thank you to my book publishing team and coach, Hilary Jastram, for bringing this book to life.

Thank you to my business coach and mentor, Tomas Keenan, for always believing in me.

Thank you to my brother and mentor, Kris Whitehead, for always pushing me to be better.

Thank you to my business partner, Marc Zalmanoff, for not only seeing the vision but helping bring it to life.

Thank you to my wife, Renée Lautermilch, for helping me every step of the way. We did it!

And thank you to all my clients who have put their trust in me to help them go get what you're worth. We're just getting warmed up!

ABOUT THE AUTHOR

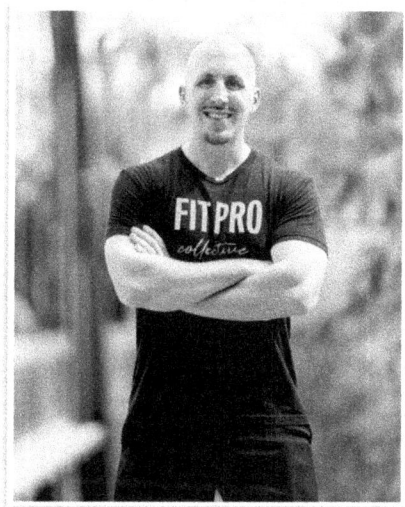

Jonathan Lautermilch is the Owner and Founder of Smart Shark and Co-Owner and Co-Founder of Fit Pro Collective. His mission in life is to help as many Fit Pros as possible get paid what they're worth.

Jonathan has 13 years of fitness industry experience, has written two books, over one hundred blogs, and is a co-host on the *Real Talk With Real Fit Pros* Podcast.

Throughout his career, Jonathan has helped thousands of Fit Pros create thriving careers and businesses within the fitness industry. He's also a loving husband and lives in Dallas, Texas.

DISCLAIMER

While the author and publisher have used their best efforts in preparing this book to provide accurate information, they make no representations or warranties with respect to the accuracy or completeness of the contents.

The advice and strategies contained herein may not be suitable for your situation and are merely the opinion of the author. Consult with a professional where appropriate.

The author and publisher specifically disclaim any liability, loss, or risk, whether personal, financial, or otherwise, that is incurred as a direct or indirect consequence from the use and/or application of any contents or material of this book and/or its resources.

The purchaser and/or reader of this publication assumes all responsibility and liability for the use of these materials and information.

Adherence to all applicable laws and regulations, both advertising and all other aspects of doing business in the United States or any other jurisdiction are the sole responsibility of the purchaser and/or reader.

www.ingramcontent.com/pod-product-compliance
Lightning Source LLC
Chambersburg PA
CBHW060618210326
41520CB00010B/1386